Too Good To Be Free

How a Reverse Mortgage Can Improve Your Life,
Your Cash Flow, and Pay You Too

Jarred J. Talmadge, MBA
Three Feet Publishing 2020

Too Good To Be Free

First Printing: 2020

ISBN 978-0-578-68600-4

Three Feet Publishing
Highlands Ranch, CO 80129

Ordering Information:

Special discounts are available on quantity purchases by corporations, associations, educators and others. For details, contact the publisher at the contact information at Three Feet Publishing, Tel: 303-257-6246, or email: ThreeFeetPublishing2020@gmail.com

US trade bookstores and wholesalers: Please contact Three Feet Publishing, Tel: 303-257-6246, or email: ThreeFeetPublishing2020@gmail.com

Too Good To Be Free

Too Good To Be Free

How a Reverse Mortgage Can Improve Your Life,
Your Cash Flow, and Pay You Too

Jarred J. Talmadge, MBA
Three Feet Publishing 2020

ACKNOWLEDGEMENTS...2

SECTION 1: PREFACE..4

SECTION 2: I HATE YOU! 6

SECTION 3: BAD NAME/COOL CONCEPT 11

SECTION 4: TOO GOOD TO BE TRUE 13

SECTION 5: REVERSE MORTGAGE MYTHS 15

SECTION 6: TRADITIONAL VS. REVERSE MORTGAGES.........18

SECTION 7: WHEN A REVERSE MORTGAGE IS THE RIGHT
OPTION 22

SECTION 8: WHEN A REVERSE MORTGAGE IS A WRONG
OPTION 34

SECTION 9: INTEREST RATES DETERMINE STRUCTURE 36

SECTION 10: INCOME AND LESA 42

SECTION 11: FAQS 46

SECTION 12: RED FLAG LOOK-OUTS 83

SECTION 13: PREPARING FOR AN APPRAISAL 86

SECTION 14: STEP-BY-STEP GUIDANCE 90

SECTION 15: AFTER CLOSING 94

SECTION 16: IN CONCLUSION..106

GLOSSARY 108

ABOUT THE AUTHOR 114

A reverse mortgage

Isn't too good to be true.

It's too good to be free.

-Jarred J. Talmadge

ACKNOWLEDGEMENTS

No huge effort can be undertaken without a village to back you up.

Thank you to my wife Bernadine. I love you. Without you, this would have never been possible.

I would like to thank my mom, Sandy Frey. Your unwavering support of Bernadine and me has made all the difference in being able to see this project through. I love you.

I also want to thank my editor, Anna Rogers. You have been amazing. You have transformed this manuscript into a book beyond my wildest imagination and I couldn't have done it without you.

I need to acknowledge three amazing people who were critical in the development of this book. Without their help learning the ropes of the reverse mortgage business, I couldn't have written anything. A huge thank you to my business coaches Kelly Rogers, Amber Adair Rasmussen and Agavni Glukhovskiy.

I would like to thank the following people who helped me in the creation of this book:

- Richard and Barbara Talmadge
- Dennis Loxton
- Ryan Zaro
- Scott Harkless
- Jesse Allen
- Tony Cavalier
- Mike Proctor
- Tyler Bohn
- Jill Wardrop
- Kathy Nickerson
- Ben Bunte
- Marcus Boswell

For Bernadine
When riches come…

SECTION 1: PREFACE

Chances are you have heard one of the horror stories in the news. Stories about how the *little, old lady* is thrown onto the street after a lifetime of paying a mortgage, all because she chose the path of a reverse mortgage. The story likely goes into great detail about how the woman was "just trying to get by" when some greasy shyster came along and took advantage of her, stole her equity, and left her homeless. Sound familiar?

When these tales are all the public hears, it is no wonder a reverse mortgage sounds so terrifying. Imagine being a senior and the one asset you view as **security** is ripped away. The fear of being alone and at the mercy of the bank can be terrifying.

This Reference Guide was put together to provide the TRUTH in a simply-stated fashion.

Did you know that in almost every, single one of the horror stories, there is ZERO accounting for all the events that occurred before the intoxicating headlines became public? The public does NOT hear about seniors not paying the taxes on the property. The public does NOT hear about the county or lender trying to remedy situations or prevent the worst from happening. The public does NOT hear those headlines because they simply don't make for juicy stories.

I used to believe the media about reverse mortgages. I thought they were scams designed to take homes from older, perhaps more vulnerable people. However, I educated myself and found that the benefits of a reverse mortgage were immense! I wanted my family members to know about this "best kept secret" and then my friends… When you care about people, you want the best for them. That is how my journey started. I believed in this opportunity so much that I found myself working for an amazing company that actually specializes in reverse mortgages. Quite a perspective shift!

Again, this reference guide was put together to provide the TRUTH in a simply-stated fashion. I have compiled some facts, figures, and some fascinating success stories. I hope to inspire you to dream, believe in hope for the future, and truly feel educated about the reverse mortgage process.

1

---

[1] *Throughout the guide, I use the term *reverse mortgage*. The legal name for a reverse mortgage is **HECM or Home Equity Conversion Mortgage**. Similarly, the term *Reverse for Purchase*, is legally **Home Equity Conversion Mortgage for Purchase**. I use the terms interchangeably, mainly because it is just so darned confusing for people.

SECTION 2: I HATE YOU!

When Dave, a financial planner, answered his phone, he wasn't expecting the first words out of the caller's mouth to be 'I hate you!' It wasn't in jest. There wasn't an inkling of sarcasm.

The caller launched into a tirade, berating Dave over some advice he had freely bestowed on the stranger while out and about the previous week. He had given the stranger a card and didn't think much would come of it. What the heck was happening? How had such an innocent transaction led to this?

Dave, an avid collector, was in California for a funeral but in his down time, he was on the lookout for some antiques. He responded to an online ad, and went to see a gentleman's collection, hoping to find a treasure. As he looked through the items, he couldn't help but notice the striking photographs on the walls.

It was a modest home that sat in the shade of a freeway overpass, but it had fallen into disrepair. Yet despite the size and condition, the walls were immaculate, thanks to frame after frame of remarkable black and white photography. Dave inquired about the artist and discovered that the owner of the home was in fact the artist. He shared with Dave that he had spent his lifetime traveling to exotic locations around the world, and that photography was a deep passion for him. There were pictures of animals in the wild on the Serengeti in Africa. There were shots of castles over the Rhine River in Germany. There were numerous shots of capitals from across the world. It was truly a site to behold.

Dave asked the man if he still traveled and was surprised to hear an emphatic NO. When pressed on why, the man shared that with the taxes and insurance on his property, he was barely getting by on his pension and social security. He further explained, that he would love to travel again, and spend his retirement photographing the different parts of the world, but knew it wasn't going to happen.

This is where Dave decided to offer a card and some free advice that would lead to the hateful call.

Dave asked the man what he thought his house was worth and he estimated $750.000. The house was located in Silicon Valley and Dave knew that even a rundown house built in the shadow of the freeway might be worth something.

Here is how the conversation went:

Dave: *If you could live anywhere, where would you go?*

Colorado sounds nice. I like the idea of living in the mountains.

Dave: *If your home is actually worth $750,000, a reverse mortgage could completely change your world.*

I've owned this home since before the freeway was built. While my home may not seem like much, it is free and clear of any mortgage. With the rising costs of real estate, especially in California, I've resigned myself to the fact that I will living here for the rest of my life. After paying the taxes and insurance on the property, it leaves little to nothing for me to live on. I am actually selling these collectables for money to live on.

Dave: *A reverse mortgage can be used to purchase a new home. If you sold your home for $750,000, you could net approximately $700,000 after commissions and fees. In the industry, it's known as a 'HECM for Purchase.' Most people do not know you can do this. Because of your age and a few other factors, you could most likely purchase a home for $500,000 but if you use a reverse mortgage for purchase, you would only have to put down around $250,000. Doing a large down payment (between 50 and 60%) means that you could live in that home for the rest of your life, without a mortgage payment. You would be responsible for taxes and insurance, as well as maintenance, but you would not have a mortgage payment!*

The seed had been planted. The business card Dave presented, and that short conversation was all it took to spur the hateful call that came two days later.

On the call the gentleman from California told Dave he had spent the rest of the weekend sitting in front of his computer, looking at homes all over the country, dreaming about what he could buy for $500,000. He went on to explain that he hated Dave because he just could not believe that the process was REAL. How dare Dave make him dream?

- A home sells for $750,000
- From the proceeds, (approximately $700,000) put $250,000 down on a new home
- That leaves him $450,000 in cash

Between his social security and his pension, plus $450,000, he would be able to afford the new place, and have money in the bank to do with as he pleased. The best part of the entire process is no mortgage payment! It's no wonder it took the man a couple of days to digest and process this. The man did sell his home. He now lives in Colorado and he travels the world pursuing his photograph and Dave now manages his money.

Can reverse mortgages change the world? Maybe. Are YOU dreaming yet???

SECTION 3: BAD NAME/COOL CONCEPT

People either love or hate the reverse mortgage industry. We have been influenced/told to hate it. Whether it be an acquaintance telling half-fact stories or the media's rating-hungry, horror stories, negative connotations swirl around the subject.

I have heard some horror stories, myself…

> ➤ People have told me they were giving away their home, so the bank can take it from them later.
> ➤ People have reported that they are selling their home to the bank, so they can live, but their heirs get NOTHING.
> ➤ People have told me that debt is "evil" and therefore by extension, a reverse mortgage is "evil."

Every one of these explanations are horribly inaccurate. The bank does not want your home. Their goal is not to take your home. When a bank goes into foreclosure on a home, it is because everything else they have tried has failed. Reverse mortgage comes down to… cash flow.

The program was designed to help seniors (over the age of 62) who own their homes, free up or create cash flow for the rest of their lives. As I said, it's not too good to be true, it's too good to be free. There **IS** a cost involved.

Bankers are not known for being risk-takers. This has not changed throughout time, so why should we expect anything different now? Bankers figured out a way to make money <u>while</u> helping people. I know, it's a crazy concept. On that note, however, this is also why many banks got out of the industry years ago, because it is not in a banker's nature to function in uncertainty. At the heart of the reverse mortgage, is an agreement that the lender will loan you money for an undetermined amount of time, in exchange for a rate of return on that money. The only way this differs from a traditional mortgage is the lender does not know when they are going to be paid back. Because the mortgage isn't due and payable until after the last borrower passes away, chances are the banker that provides the loan today, will be retired by the time the loan is actually paid off. It is a lifetime of risk for the bank and as a result, they charge for it. Hopefully now you understand why I always say:

**A reverse mortgage
Isn't too good to be true.
It's too good to be free.**
-Jarred J. Talmadge

The first question I am continuously asked when presenting the concept of a reverse mortgage, is,

"Isn't this too good to be true?"

My answer is always the same. *No!* Next, my ever-growing popular phrase follows, *"It's not too good to be true, it's too good to be free."*

The reverse mortgage is not that different from any other FHA-backed government loan. All FHA (Federal Housing Administration) loans require people to carry mortgage insurance and have at least some level of equity in their property. Most importantly, these are intended to help people acquire mortgages that banks may not favor. The most common FHA loans are those that provide down payment assistance for first-time homebuyers with as little as 3% down.

Simplified here: On a $100,000 loan, one could put down 3% or 3.5% and the bank will lend the rest. When purchasing a home thirty or forty years ago, one would have been required to put 20% down. But putting down $3,500 vs. $20,000 would make a big difference when buying a home. There **IS** a risk to the bank though. It is significantly more dangerous for the bank to lend to someone who only puts down 3%, as opposed to someone putting down, 20%. Because of this, the banker's fallback position is usually the word NO. They will not do those type of loans because of the risk of likely default.

FHA recognized this as a problem, so they stepped in to guarantee the bank payments. Simply stated, if these loans defaulted, FHA pays them off, and the bank accrues no further risk. This plan worked wonderfully for first-time homebuyers who were usually young without enough money saved to purchase a house. The question soon became, *Why couldn't we do this for the other end of the spectrum too? Can't we help seniors as well?* The answer was a resounding *YES*! FHA can, and they do now help seniors. It is not called down payment assistance. It is called a reverse mortgage.

Before diving too deeply into reverse mortgage details, let's address some of the myths that are floating around about the reverse mortgage industry.

Myth #1: *The lender will own my home, or I am selling my home for some of the equity.*	I am convinced this is a tale told by lenders who do not sell reverse mortgages.

As the borrower, you retain ownership of your home as long as you comply with the loan terms and conditions. It is usually quite simple. Your home has to be your <u>primary</u> residence: lived in for six months and one day out of every year. You also will pay the taxes and maintain the homeowner's insurance.

Myth #2: *I can no longer sell my home.*	Just like a traditional mortgage, you are free to sell your home whenever you want.

When you do sell your home, you must pay off the reverse mortgage. Take the sales price, subtract what is owed on the mortgage and pocket the rest. Pre-payment penalties are prohibited, so there is a NO penalty to pay for selling your home.

Myth #3: My heirs will have nothing but my debt to inherit.	Your heirs have options.

Your heirs can pay off the loan balance and keep the home. If there is equity (there usually is) your heirs may access that as well. They can sell the property if the desire and acquire the remaining equity. If you happen to pass away owing more than the home is worth, FHA will pay off the difference, and your heirs don't inherit your debt.

Myth #4: Reverse mortgage is only a last resort for seniors without any assets.	Everyone can benefit from better cash flow.

There are plenty of wealthy seniors choosing to enhance their retirement strategies with reverse mortgages.

Myth #5: Once the loan proceeds are received, I pay taxes on them.	Reverse mortgage proceeds are paid out tax-free as they are not considered income by the IRS.

Reverse mortgages do not affect social security or Medicare, and they are not taxable, according to the IRS.

Myth #6: The home must be free and clear of any existing mortgages.	Usually you need to have equity in your home- around 50% or more.

Note: if you have an existing mortgage, the reverse mortgage will pay off the existing mortgage and eliminate required monthly mortgage payments, if you have enough equity.

Myth #7: The fees for a reverse are high.	Reverse mortgage fees are competitive with any other government-backed financing options.

I hope some of the old wives' tales got cleared up. Now let's dig deeper into the reverse mortgage world. Are you still dreaming?

SECTION 6: TRADITIONAL VS. REVERSE MORTGAGES

All one has to do is mention *mortgage* or *interest rates* and everyone and their brother automatically become experts. People argue at great length between the proper use of their, there, and they're. But when it comes to mortgage lending, everyone thinks they are an expert. One of the tell-tale signs that someone is an amateur in the field (has no business offering advice on the subject) is when he or she starts arguing about rates above everything else.

Credit scores are usually based on a scale of 350 to 850. Scores on the extreme ends are rare. In twenty-four years of lending, I can count only a handful of occurrences of credit scores under 400. In fact, going through a bankruptcy or foreclosure will not put someone's credit score that low. Similarly, scores over 800 are equally as rare. The good news is that in the last year, I have seen more 800+ credit scores than I have in twenty-four years of lending.

I received an email from a client who was going through the lending process. She had great credit. She stated that interest rates were down and that she was *getting an offer* at 3.5%. The hairs on the back of my neck started to stand on end. Here is what I know. Shopping for interest rates on reverse mortgages is not the same as shopping for forward/traditional mortgages.

When shopping for a forward mortgage, usually people focus on interest rates, assuming the lowest number is the best. Nothing could be further from the truth. There are several factors to consider when shopping for interest rates so do not simply focus on that one aspect if you truly want the best possible deal. Here is an example.

Sherry was being quoted 3.5% on a mortgage. That sounds really good right? What about the fees? I want to know how long the rate lock is in place. I also want to know if the company is credible. Here's why.

NO ONE FINANCES ANYTHING FOR FREE.

Even those 0% interest programs are not technically free. The lender is making money. Usually, in the case of 0% offers, the lender is making money in other ways. Whether that means paying more in interest later on or selling someone's information, rest assured that lenders make money. The other reason companies offer 0% interest is that most people, when given that choice, will buy anything with the intention of paying it off before the offer ends. However, what usually gets divulged when people read the fine print, is that the interest is actually retroactive (back to the day the purchase was made) if the balance is not payed off in the required timeframe. What happens? Most people don't pay in time and get hit with retroactive fees and pay 21% interest from day one.

Now it does not look like such a great deal.

Financing a mortgage is not exactly the same. Beating the lender up to get a better rate means the lender is going to find other ways to make their money, often times where you do not see. Wow! But wait! There is more! Any lender can tell you they can give you a better rate. The issue is the attachment of **fees**. The client may get a lower rate, but what are the fees?

Take the case of the 3.5% mortgage story I previously touched on. The client contacted me because she wanted a lower rate. The deal I got for her is 3.99%, a difference of half a point of interest. What she did not realize was that I also gave her a great deal on the fees. How do you combat this? The best way to handle anything along these lines is to ask for something in writing. With all the regulations covering mortgages, there is a specific way in which the lender must present the fees. *Anyone can say anything* but when you ask to have it put in writing, the rubber meets the road. If you want to compare apples to apples, you need something in writing. This practice will tell you if the rate is really as good as you think it is.

THE RULES ARE DIFFERENT

The rules for interest rates on reverse mortgages are different from traditional mortgages. Because of this, how you ask the questions about interest rates need to be different as well. With reverse mortgages, the rate cannot be locked in until just-before the loan closes.

There is not a "lock" available on a reverse mortgage. *Lock*, meaning a guaranteed, rate for a certain period, as with forward mortgages. Interest rates move all the time (sometimes multiple times a day), depending on what happens with the economy. In the reverse mortgage world, the only guarantee of a rate is the word of your lender. One can clearly see why it is important to trust your lender.

Like most companies, the one I work for has a reputation to defend. We want to be viewed as reputable. As a result, if we say we are going to do something, we do it. Again, it is clear why having a written record of everything is vital!

Summing this up, the Russians have a saying for this: Doveryai no proberyai. It means: Trust but verify.

Section 7: When a Reverse Mortgage is the Right Option

As most know, being rich does NOT solve life's problems. However, being rich does mean that a person has more money to help solve life's problems.

A reverse mortgage will not make you rich. A reverse mortgage will not make you poor either. As I learned in graduate school, having money doesn't make someone rich; cash flow does.

How Does Cash Flow Make You Rich?

Being rich means sitting on a pile of money. Picture the old cartoon with Scrooge McDuck. Scrooge sits in his vault and swims through his gold coins. He doesn't seem to do anything, yet swimming through his money seems to make him happy. I pose this question. What happens if he runs out of money?

The myth of wealth in America is that if someone is a millionaire, he or she is doing well, yet we know plenty of millionaires that are miserable. They worry all the time that their money is going to disappear, and they will never be able to make it again. Why? It's not money that makes people rich. Cash flow makes people rich. The ability to have money replenished at the beginning of each month is HUGE! Simply put, a reverse mortgage will not make someone rich, but it **will** improve cash flow!

Right now, as this book is being written, the Corona Virus is closing down the country. People are missing paychecks and falling behind. It's because they don't have cash flow. If they have savings, they are burning through them. This is why cash flow is so vitally important and this is why a reverse mortgage is a perfect solution.

In the reverse mortgage industry, there is a dividing line:

Before October 2017 -------------------- After October 2017

In October of 2017, the rules around reverse mortgage changed. Prior to that date, the reverse mortgage field was largely unregulated. Lenders were free to lend as much as their risk-tolerance would handle. This meant that if a lender wanted to give someone 100% of what their house was worth, whether a smart move for the individual or not, they could do what they wanted.

Thankfully, the government stepped in, changed the rules, and regulated the reverse mortgage industry in October 2017. The rules for reverse mortgage became simple: If someone wants a reverse mortgage, the lender must prove:

- ✓ He or she can maintain the home.
- ✓ He or she can pay the taxes and insurance.
- ✓ That the loan is beneficial for the individual.

The industry no longer centers around what is good for the lender. Instead, it is about what is best for the consumer.

When speaking with seniors, one of the biggest problems reported is lack of cash flow. Having equity in a home is great. Spending a lifetime investing in a home and paying off the mortgage is commendable, yet many seniors find that the promise of a paid-off home is not enough to keep a proper, monthly cash flow. Many seniors end up spending an inordinate amount of money on mortgage payments each month, which does not leave enough to live on. If this doesn't seem like the antithesis of the American dream, I do not know what does. This is why the reverse mortgage was created.

> *The equity you have accumulated in your home is a direct result of you paying off your mortgage combined with an increase in the value of your home. It's confirmation that you made a good decision to purchase the home, maintain it, and pay it off. Why shouldn't you be able to access it?*

NOW, you have the option of getting access to your equity in four ways:

1. A lump sum of money at closing (1 time only) or
2. Monthly payments to you, or
3. Access it as a line of credit to be used as needed or
4. A combination of a few of these together.

The fear of running out of money is very real. I have a client named Tina who made around $2,000 a month between social security and pension. Tina's mortgage payments were $1,300 a month. After adding in taxes and insurance, she was strapped for cash.

She expressed fear of a future emergency, not having enough cash to live on, and no savings. Living without even the smallest of safety nets is scary. Imagine barely squeaking by on $500 a month. The fear can be debilitating.

Thankfully, Tina had enough equity in her home, that she could utilize a reverse mortgage. In her case, a reverse mortgage allowed her to wipe out existing mortgages and free up cash. Instead of a $1,300 mortgage payment every month, she now merely needs to have $200 for taxes and insurance each month. That is a net savings of at least $1,100 a month. $1,600 a month cash flow instead of $500. Life completely changed for Tina! She could even dream again.

One of the most popular features of a reverse mortgage is the line of credit feature. This feature is especially beneficial if you do not need the money right away and you are young enough to take advantage of it over time. Here is an example of how it works:

I was working with a friend of my mom's named Dawn who had just celebrated her 62nd birthday. She did not need money right away but had a mortgage payment. She was still working, so making the mortgage payment was "no big deal." However, I learned she did not owe very much on her mortgage so I suggested she should look into a reverse mortgage, not out of necessity, but rather as an investment in her future. This threw her for a loop. Her first question, as I am sure yours is too, was

Why take out a reverse mortgage if I don't _need_ *it?*

I explained that *right now* she may not need it, but asked what twenty years later would look like? If she were to take out a reverse mortgage to pay off the existing mortgage, it cancels her first mortgage, and with it, the mortgage payment. Dawn was very capable of making her taxes and insurance payments from her salary and she had assets. I assured her that if ever there was someone who the bank **wanted** to lend to, it would be her. If she paid off the first mortgage there would be no more payments but now she would owe money on the reverse mortgage. The advantage is that she would obtain a line of credit attached to the house and through time, as her home appreciates, the line of credit would GROW!

A REVERSE LINE OF CREDIT IS DIFFERENT

When I told Dawn, we should set her up on a line of credit, I was suggesting it because she didn't need it. Remember, she owed a little bit of money on her mortgage. We paid that off with the reverse mortgage. The line of credit gave her access to her money. She got a form from the company which she simply uses to send in with her request when she needs money from here on out. Within a couple of days, money appears in her account and she is free to use it for whatever she wants.

Remember though, Dawn did NOT need the money. Instead of using it, she could simply let it *sit there*, let's say for twenty years. What happens to the line of credit? It grows- approximately 5% a year, for twenty years!

Here is the math. Let's say Dawn has a $200,000 line of credit at the time she starts her reverse mortgage at the age of sixty-two. The line of credit is like a credit card. If you do not use it, you do not pay interest on it. Let's run that info through twenty years and see how it grows.

Year	1	$200,000
Year	2	$210,000
Year	3	$220,500
Year	4	$231,525
Year	5	$243,101
Year	6	$255,256

Year	7	$268,019
Year	8	$281,420
Year	9	$295,491
Year	10	$310,266
Year	11	$325,779
Year	12	$342,068
Year	13	$359,171
Year	14	$377,130
Year	15	$395,986
Year	16	$415,786
Year	17	$436,575
Year	18	$458,404
Year	19	$481,324
Year	20	$505,390

Look at what happens! The line of credit grows to $505,390 in twenty years!

Next, let us assume Dawn needs assistance to stay in her home when she is 82. Now she has options. She could tap money from her 401K or retirement savings or, she could use some of the money from her reverse mortgage to pay for anything she needs. She can get it in a matter of days. She does not have to ask permission or apply for a loan. It is there and available. How cool is that?

Compare that to a home equity loan. If she needed help at age 82, would she make enough money to qualify for a bank to loan money? The answer is probably not.

ANOTHER WAY TO USE A REVERSE MORTGAGE:

Using the same example of the $200,000 line of credit that grows to $505,390, what if Dawn invested in the stock market, which moves up and down? What happens if she needs some money during one of those down years? Should she take it out of the stock market? Not necessarily. She could take it out of the line of credit, instead of taking it out of her nest egg. The last thing anyone would want to do is take money out of the stock market when the stock market is down. Why? Because taking money out of a stock account reduces the amount of money that is working for you. As a result, you do not give your money time to recover from the poor market. Furthermore, there might be tax implications or penalties. (For the record, I am not a financial planner and I don't play one on TV either.)

If you spend your money, it won't work for you in the future.

THE KIDS WILL BE OKAY

One of the most common misconceptions about obtaining a reverse mortgage is that there will be nothing to leave any heirs. While that may have been true in the past, it is not anymore. The way the reverse mortgage is structured, there will be equity left most of the time.

Before 2017, lenders were free to lend up to their *risk-tolerance*. In other words, if the lender wanted to lend 90% of what a home was worth and the clients were okay with it, so be it. Lenders cannot do this anymore. Since October of 2017, new rules have been established which do not allow lenders to give that much equity. As a result, a lot of lenders and loan officers left the business. The easy money was gone. It was no longer the *wild west* of mortgage lending.

If making the decision to take out a reverse mortgage, one would still have equity left over after passing away.

THE PROGRAM IS DESIGNED TO LEAVE PEOPLE EQUITY.

The new maximum lending amounts will rarely allow people to borrow more than 70% of their equity. Usually, that number is closer to 50% - 60%. First, as the borrower, it gives you options. Many people misunderstand the reverse mortgage because they think they are trading their home for a reduced amount of equity. However, that is not how it works. As previously stated, when you take out a reverse mortgage, you are not giving up your equity.

Think of it this way:

Say your home is worth $100

A reverse mortgage will allow you to borrow $40 and give you a line of credit of $10.

As your home value appreciates, you may find your home value at $150.

Depending on how you set up your reverse mortgage, you have a $40 line of credit and your original reverse mortgage may have grown to $55.

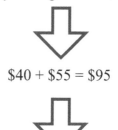

$40 + $55 = $95

If your home is worth $150, that means you could sell it, pay off everything you owe ($95), and still have money left over ($55).

WHY STRUGGLE?

Think about any possible heirs for a moment. What are they going to want from you? If you have the opportunity to tap into equity in your home to make life better, would they want that for you?

When most people inherit a home, they end up selling it. Why? Because inheritors have their own lives and their own homes. They do not want to uproot the family and move into a different neighborhood. To be blunt, most just want the money. Here is the hard-hitting question. Would your heirs be happy with less money, if it ensured that YOU were taken care of?

What could you do with the money?

There are generally three categories that most people fall into.

1. Immediate Needs
2. Improvement of Lifestyle
3. Planning

The first category of people are those who have an immediate need for cash. Health care services, education for grandchildren, and/or investment opportunities seem to be common reasons. Regardless of what you may want cash for, it is your money to use as you please.

The second category of people are those who want to improve their lifestyles. This may mean lowering the cost of living by getting rid of the mortgage payments. There is never anything wrong with improving cash flow.

I've known people who used the money to make improvements to their homes, while others want to use the money to buy a second home.

Finally, the third category are those who are planners. These seem to be the rarest of people. Planners are usually well informed and understand how to use tax-free money to their benefit. They also understand the power of having a pool of money to draw from, rather than taking money out of the stock market in a situation where they would potentially be taking a loss. Instead, they dip into the reverse mortgage and give their stocks time to recover. This way they still maintain the money they need to live on, and lifestyles are not affected.

Others see it as an ongoing emergency line of credit, that they can tap into on quick notice if needed.

SECTION 8: WHEN A REVERSE MORTGAGE IS A WRONG OPTION

There are times when a reverse mortgage is not a good idea.

SELLING SOON

If you are planning to sell your home soon (within two to five years), a reverse mortgage would not be the wisest decision. Reverse mortgages generally have fees associated with them. One of these fees is mortgage insurance. The mortgage insurance premium is usually 2% of the value of the home being refinanced into a reverse mortgage, up to $12,000.

Mortgage insurance is part of <u>most</u> reverse mortgages. It's not something that can be negotiated, waived, or credited. It is part of the deal. The fee is usually paid up front and included in the loan. What if you found yourself having to move after taking out a reverse mortgage. Once including mortgage insurance in the fees, it adds up. You will save more if you **do not do** a reverse mortgage.

When taking out a traditional mortgage, there is a known end date (15 years or 30 years). Because it is know when the mortgage will end, one can figure out the cost of the loan divided over the period of time. With a reverse mortgage, one does NOT know how long it lasts, but the less time had, the more expensive it is, relative to what is borrowed.

NO BENEFIT

One of the helpful modifications after 2017 was the requirement that the mortgage <u>must benefit the client</u>. Prior to that, a reverse mortgage did not have to benefit the consumer. There is now a requirement for ***financial benefit***, in order for mortgages to be approved by HUD. This protects people from predatory lenders.

LEAVE THE HOME FREE AND CLEAR

A reverse mortgage is not a good idea if you want to leave your home to an heir, free and clear. If you take out a reverse mortgage, your home is not *free and clear*.

Most people want to leave their heirs something. A reverse mortgage allows you to leave some equity in your home as your legacy, but it does not take all of it. You are still leaving some equity to your heirs. At the same time, you are getting the benefit of it in your lifetime.

SECTION 9: INTEREST RATES DETERMINE STRUCTURE

The reverse mortgage world is different from the traditional mortgage world and it is never more apparent than when discussing interest rates.

Most people want a fixed rate mortgage. It is easy to see why. Every month, the mortgage is the same. If you are looking at a thirty-year commitment, and you know you can pay the mortgage now, there is a good chance as you advance in your career; you can still afford it later.

The reverse mortgage world is different. The way a loan is structured, will determine how one can access money. In complete contrast to the traditional mortgage world, the most popular reverse mortgages are <u>adjustable rate</u> mortgages. You may be thinking, *that doesn't make any sense, don't most people want a fixed rate for all the reasons you listed above*? The answer is usually yes, until the client gets an education in reverse mortgages.

With a reverse mortgage, payments are not the driving factor, since people are not required to ever make payments. There are significant advantages to an adjustable rate mortgage on a reverse mortgage. With an adjustable rate, you will have access to part of your equity at closing (40% of the available funds) and the rest one year and one day later. (the remaining 60% of available funds less what is owed on the home at the time of closing.)

With a fixed rate reverse mortgage, there is only one draw period. You can get as much equity as you can at the time of closing the loan file, no more can be withdrawn unless there is a refinance.

If you want the most money **now** and do not want to worry about taking out cash later, a fixed rate reverse mortgage is your best bet. If you want more options for getting money in the future, an adjustable rate mortgage is best.

Fixed vs. Adjustable: The real difference

When it comes to a reverse mortgage, the difference between a fixed rate and an adjustable rate mortgage goes well beyond the interest rates. It is all about the benefits. Most of my clients still think they want a fixed rate mortgage when they start the process of getting a reverse mortgage. However, once we start talking about the differences, their opinions quickly change. I will explain here, what I explain to my clients about the differences.

A Fixed Rate Reverse Mortgage:

Just like a traditional mortgage, on a fixed rate reverse mortgage, the interest rate never changes. You can look at an amortization schedule and can see what you will owe, what your balance will be through time, and how much your house is worth. A fixed rate reverse mortgage allows you to know at closing that you can take out a specific amount of equity. Fixed rate reverse mortgages will only allow to borrow your equity once.

When applying for a reverse mortgage and indicating you want a fixed rate, the lender will tell you how much money you can borrow. Just like your interest rate, that number is fixed. Once you complete the transaction, you will not have to make mortgage payments in your lifetime.

However, if for some reason in the future you want to borrow more money (maybe because your equity went up significantly) you would have to refinance and pay fees again. You may be thinking, *well that doesn't sound too bad*. It is not. If you are in a situation where you want a one-time advance of money and the peace of mind knowing your interest rate is fixed, then a fixed rate reverse mortgage may be your best option.

Adjustable Rate Mortgage:

The adjustable rate mortgage is the more popular option. The reason for this is simple flexibility. Not flexibility in the rate, but rather in how one can access equity. If you want the most money out of your home right now, a fixed rate reverse mortgage is your best bet. However, if you want some options in the future, an adjustable rate mortgage is the right one for you.

An adjustable rate reverse mortgage gives you more options on how you would like your money. The most common way people access their equity, is to utilize a line of credit.

With an adjustable rate reverse mortgage, you usually have access to part of your money when you close. An adjustable rate mortgage can also give you access to more of your equity one year and one day later in the form of a line of credit.

How the line of credit works is that you have access to some of your equity at closing. You have the option to pass and leave it on a line of credit that you can access later.

One year and one day later, you should see the first increase. Then, as long as you don't use all of the line of credit, the line of credit will grow every year.

Here is where an adjustable rate mortgage really makes sense. Think of the line of credit like a credit card. Let's say, you have access to $50,000 at closing, but you don't need it.

You let it sit there.

A year later, you have an increase of $100,000. Remember, you did not use the $50,000 from year one. By year two, that line of credit is now $150,000. Again, you do not use it. That line of credit will grow every year, at approximately 5% a year. The less you use it, the faster it will grow. This becomes significant in the years after you take out the reverse mortgage. By letting that line of credit sit, you allow it to grow. As your home gets more valuable, your line of credit grows too.

If you took out a reverse mortgage at sixty-two and let the line of credit sit for 20 years, it would grow to approximately $361,000 by year twenty. What would happen if at the age of eighty-two, you needed in-home health care? What if you needed money for something else? Look at the advantage of having a reverse mortgage with an adjustable rate:

If you tried to apply for a traditional mortgage at age eighty-two, the lender is going to for proof of income. If you are only making social security, chances are you won't have enough income to borrow anything, right? If you have a HELOC (Home Equity Line of Credit), you can borrow on that line of credit, but you have to pay it back and make payments. If you are on a limited income, this is a problem.

However, in this same situation, with the reverse mortgage that you have let sit for 20 years, you have access to a line of credit worth $361,000. To access that line of credit, all you would have to do is contact the lender and tell them you want to advance money.

Consider that if you were taking money out of a 401K or a stock account, you are going to pay taxes on what you take out. In addition, by taking out money, it is no longer working for you and you risk the chance of depleting your savings.

With the reverse mortgage, you have that line of credit to draw from which would allow you to keep any nest egg intact. There are no taxes withheld, because you are borrowing your own money. In addition, you can get access to it within a few days, without having to justify the use. You simply make a request and a few days later, it shows up.

Talk about peace of mind. Imagine knowing that you have more than you need and that you can make you money last longer! The real question becomes, how much is that peace of mind worth? I hope that it is clear why the adjustable rate reverse mortgage is so popular.

SECTION 10: INCOME AND LESA

The reverse mortgage is not driven by income. Simply put, your income is not the sole determining factor in whether you get a reverse mortgage or not. You will still be asked to prove an income (Most clients receive social security, a pension and/or have retirement savings). Traditional banks and lenders are going to want to see income for paying back the loan. With a reverse mortgage, you will need to verify that you can pay your taxes, insurance, and have money left over to live on. The traditional mortgage will ask for bank statements, tax records, W2 forms, and will look at your expenses to determine if you spend too much. With reverse mortgages, you are asked to have income and go through a Financial Assessment.

This is a government-mandated test to make sure you can even take advantage of a reverse mortgage. The financial assessment is usually a pass or fail situation. You are asked some simple questions about your lifestyle, income, and assets. If you fail the financial assessment, it does not mean you cannot get a reverse mortgage. It just means the process will be a little more complicated because it you do not have enough income to pay tax and insurance costs every month.

With a reverse mortgage you will still need to provide the lender with proof of your income and assets. Usually a social security award letter and a couple of months of bank statements and/or asset statements will do it.

Every negative story I have ever heard about reverse mortgage comes from before 2017 and <u>the lack of a financial assessment</u>. There was an article in a major newspaper about a grandmother in Baltimore who lost her home when she was foreclosed on by her reverse mortgage lender.

Poor grandma was sobbing on her front porch. Her belongings were all over the sidewalk and people were stealing from her. She was ranting about how the bank took advantage of her.

That was not the whole story.

The bank did NOT want her house. They never did. In this particular case, the woman borrowed all of the equity she had in her home, turned around and gave it to her grandson, who had gambling debt. She didn't have any money left over to pay her property taxes and insurance on the house. After several years, the county/state got tired of fighting and seized her home. Because she didn't understand what happened, she blamed the mortgage company.

It is very clear why financial assessments were put into place. These occurrences should never happen. The financial assessment was designed to make sure you have money left over for essentials like paying property taxes, insurance, and household bills. Since you are required to pay those yourself, lenders wants to guarantee that you are financially able, to avoid defaulting on the reverse mortgage terms.

What happens if you want a reverse mortgage and your income is so limited, that even with getting money from your equity, you don't make enough to cover your bills.

There is an answer and her name is LESA.

LESA or *Life Expectancy Set Aside* is for people who have a lot of equity in their home but may not have enough cash flow every month to pay taxes and insurance on their homes.

Say you do not pass the financial assessment but have lots of equity in your home.

A LESA acts as an escrow account for taxes and insurance for the rest of your life expectancy.

With a LESA, the lender looks at your equity and makes a calculation based on what your taxes and insurance are. Then they project it out until your mid 90's or so, based on your estimated life span. The lender can then, with reasonable accuracy, figure out how much money is needed to pay your taxes and insurance. The lender sets aside that money in an escrow account and if you decide to do the reverse mortgage, that money will be deducted from what you can borrow. The lender uses that money to pay your taxes and insurance every year, for the rest of your life. A LESA is required in several circumstances. Here is an example.

I had a client named Roger who was renting out his basement. He had more than enough money to live on with his pension and social security, but he had a basement he was not using, so he rigged his home to create a separate apartment in the basement.

By all measures, the client did everything right. He declared his income from his rental property and made sure he declared that income on his taxes.

A problem arose when he had the house appraised. The appraiser noted that he lived in a townhouse that was zoned for single-family living. Since Roger had effectively created a second apartment in his house, it was in violation of FHA renting policy. As a result, even though the client did everything right, the underwriter would not allow him to count his income from the renter. As a result, he failed the financial assessment and a LESA was required.

The LESA account would have required the lender to hold back around $40,000, which was the estimate on Roger's taxes and insurance for thirty-five years. This created a unique problem. Even though he was getting income from his renter in the basement, underwriters (decision makers) would not allow him to count it. He looked like he could not afford the home, even when he could. Roger needed a LESA account or he could not do the loan. He ended up electing not to do the deal because he did not want to set aside that much money. Was it the right decision? Who knows? But it was his decision to make.

SECTION 11: FAQS

What is Required to get a Reverse Mortgage?

- ✓ It is only available to homeowners over the age of 62
- ✓ You must own your home
- ✓ The home is your primary residence - live in the house more than six months a year.

Is the Program Limited to Single-Family Homes?

NO. You can use a reverse mortgage if you own a townhome, condominium, single-family home, duplex, triplex, or even a fourplex, as long as you live in one of the units. If you have a modular or manufactured home, it may have been built off-site and trucked into a location. As long as the home is attached to the foundation / does not move, the home may qualify.

What Are the Conditions For a Reverse Mortgage?

You need to be able to demonstrate that you can pay the taxes, insurance, homeowner's insurance dues, and still be able to have money left over. This is called the *financial assessment*. One of the big keys to getting a reverse mortgage is to demonstrate you can pay for upkeep.

What are the Mandatory Obligations?

When you start down the road of the reverse mortgage, the lender may talk about mandatory obligations. This is just industry-speak for obligations that need to be paid before the reverse mortgage can be put into place. These could be obligations like an existing mortgage or a line of credit. It could also entail a tax lien or a mechanics lien on your home. The rule of thumb is, that in order to get a reverse mortgage, these items should not exceed 50% of the value of your home. Ideally, you want to still have a good amount of money left over after the mandatory obligations are paid so you have money to pay the fees associated with your reverse mortgage. Also having money left over means you have a better chance of qualifying for a line of credit.

Why Can't I Acquire All My Equity?

One of the most common, heartbreaking questions I have to answer as Mortgage Planning Professional is, *Why can't I get all my money right now?* Throughout this guide, I talk about how it is your money and you should be able to get access to it. That being said, the reason the reverse mortgage industry works, is because you usually can't get all your money at once.

I have a client who is ninety-years-old. She owns her home free and clear, has very high credit scores, and her total debt is $50. I **STILL** had to get a pricing exception because she wanted more than 40% of her money at once. Generally, you can get 40% of your money at closing and the rest (60% of the availability) one year and one day later. There are exceptions, but they are few and far-between.

Are Reverse Mortgages Expensive?

I hate answering a question with a question, but in this case, I always ask, *In comparison to what*? Reverse mortgages have a reputation for being expensive, based on prior to 2017 issues. More often than not, the one item that stands out against everything else is one line of the fee sheet. It is the line for mortgage insurance.

Mortgage insurance is usually the most expensive cost by a country mile. Mortgage insurance should be your best friend though and here is why.

Think back to 2007 – 2008. The economy was tanking, people were losing their homes, and home values were dropping like a rock. In some places, housing prices dropped so significantly, the banks got spooked and started foreclosing in anticipation of the losses.

Imagine yourself in that time. You may have found yourself owing more than your house was worth. The bank would send you a letter, informing you that your home was now worth less than you owe, and you needed to come up with a large sum of money to bring down the mortgage or face foreclosure. How scary would that have been? It did not matter if you were going to sell or ride out the storm. The bank <u>was exposed</u>, which meant you could lose your home as a result. Enter mortgage insurance for a reverse mortgage…

When all the rules for reverse mortgage changed in 2017, one of the rules that angered many people was the addition of mortgage insurance as a requirement for loans. Up to 2% of the balance of the mortgage would be charged as mortgage insurance and an additional 0.5% would be collected monthly. This increased the cost of a reverse mortgage. The government put protections into place for homeowners that far outweigh the costs.

First, having mortgage insurance on your loan means both you and the lender are protected in case anything like the economy of 2008 happens again. It is just a matter of time before we are facing the same position again. Don't believe me?

The mortgage crisis was precipitated by lenders who saw people with less-than-perfect credit as a big piggy bank. They figured people wanted places to live, so they created programs specifically designed for them: people with bad credit. The no-income, no-asset loan was soon created. In the mortgage business, it was often referred to as a *liar loan.*

Back in the day, one could call up a mortgage broker, tell them you made $10,000 a month and that you wanted to buy a home with no down payment and no proof that you could pay. All you had to do was state that you could. If your credit was good enough, the loan was granted, without verifying anything. In 2008, companies were going bankrupt because all those loans started to default at once. Everyone swore that was the end of such customs, but guess what I saw last year? The first *liar loans* in a decade coming back. This is how to protect yourself.

Mortgage insurance acts as protection. Mortgage insurance is in place to make sure what happened in 2008, can never happen to you. It protects you, the homeowner, from a situation where your home decreases in value to the point where you might owe the lender more than your home is worth. If history repeats itself, having mortgage insurance means you are safe, as long as you live in your home. It's a guarantee from FHA that pronounces, if that ever happens, the government will pick up the difference and pay the lender back if you default or sell for less than you owe. As long as you live in your home, maintain it, pay taxes, and keep it insured, there is nothing the lender can do to take your home. Wait! There is more!

A reverse mortgage is also a non-recourse loan. This means that your home (not you or your heirs) owe the money. With a non-recourse loan, if you ever find yourself in a situation where you owe more than your home is worth, you have some options:

1. Do nothing and keep living in your home. This is truly your best option, because eventually the housing markets recover. If you can, it's best to ride it out.
2. Walk away from the home. If you absolutely have to move because you cannot afford the home, you walk away and let the home go into foreclosure. However, there is a catch.

Say you owed $150,000 and your home was worth $100,000. After Realtor fees and costs, say it sold and the bank only got $85,000 for it.

If you subtract $85,000, there is still $65,000 unaccounted for. On a traditional mortgage, you would be responsible for that difference. On a reverse mortgage, because it is a non-recourse loan, FHA covers the difference.

Here's an example. If you pass away owing more than the home is worth, your heirs can pay off the mortgage for 95% of whichever is less, the appraised value or what you owed, whichever is less.

Changes the game doesn't it?

What am I Paying For?

There is a dividing line between what you have to pay out-of-pocket now, and what you have to pay for as part of the loan. Understanding the difference will be key to feeling better about the loan transaction you are working on.

First, let's tackle out-of-pocket costs. These are costs you pay in order to complete your loan. Usually these fees are minimal, but if you are not aware of them or are not expecting them, they can be a bit startling.

FHA Counseling Fee:

One of the biggest changes after 2017 was the requirement of the FHA counseling fee. In the industry, we call this *The Golden Ticket* in reference to the winning ticket Charlie found in order to visit that famous chocolate factory. We call this the golden ticket because, just like in Charlie and the Chocolate Factory, he couldn't proceed without the golden ticket, so too mortgage lenders cannot proceed without it.

At the initial meeting, the loan officer will give you a list of FHA counseling providers. These providers are third parties who provide the counseling services. Why third parties? Prior to 2017, lenders were taking advantage of clients who did not fully comprehend the process. People were getting confused. Now it is a requirement that before you proceed to the application stage of a reverse mortgage, you must complete counseling which usually runs around $125 - $200. I always say:

"It doesn't matter to me, one way or another, which one you choose. You can choose to do it over the phone or in person. I can't have anything to do with your choice. All I ask is that you provide whomever you choose with my email address and ask them to please email a copy of the certificate to my loan officer upon completion."

Usually most companies have no problem with that. If you have a financial counselor or children who want to better understand the process, they are welcome to be on the call, or sit in on the counseling session. You are not paying per person. You are paying for the service. As a result, anyone you want to better understand the reverse mortgage should be on the call or in the appointment with you.

Why Do You (the lender) Want My Counseling Certificate? The answer is two-fold:

1. By emailing me a copy, I keep it for my files. If for some reason the document is lost, I can pull it up on my computer and send it out again.

2. Usually a wet signature (live) is required in blue ink. I print out a copy, include it in the application documents, and ask for a signature from you on the document when we meet to sign the loan application documents.

The Appraisal Cost:

The other big out-of-pocket cost is <u>the appraisal</u>. It measures your commitment to the process. An appraisal can cost anywhere from $625 to more than $1,200. Considering the lender's view, this makes sense. By asking you, the client, to pay for the appraisal before the loan is completed, the lender views this as measuring your commitment to the loan. In poker terms, it's called being 'pot committed.' Which means, by paying the appraisal cost out of pocket, you are essentially telling the lender you want to move forward with the loan. From my point of view, it's simple housekeeping.

Back when appraisals were cheap ($350), I ran a brokerage and one of our promotions was a free appraisal if you closed a loan with us. The problem with that promotion was if there was a problem with the appraisal, such as the house not appraising high enough, I was left holding the bill. I only did that a few times before realizing that maybe it was not the best way to get business.

Closing Costs:

Closing costs are different from out-of-pocket costs. Closing costs are paid at closing and are deducted from the amount of money you receive.

Here are the different closing costs and purposes.

Origination Fee	Covers the cost of processing the loan, getting documents done, and delivering the loan package for closing.
Lender Credit	If there is a lender credit, it is usually because a fee got waved and money is being refunded. Usually the lender credit appears as a negative number on the *Good Faith Estimate* document.
Appraisal Fee	Because the lender is charging a fee, it must be disclosed. This is the fee paid to the appraisal company for preparing a report to estimate the market value of your home.

Credit Report Fee	This fee is the cost the lender pays to pull a tri-merge credit report (a report that combines the information of all three major credit report companies: Experian, Trans Union, and Equifax). This is where the lender will get your credit scores, using the middle of your three scores to determine your credit.
Flood Certification	This fee is what the lender charges to determine if your home is in a floodplain. Usually, if it is, you already know and already carry flood insurance.
Tax Certificate	The document that is usually issued by the county which states you have paid property taxes and there are no current taxes due.

Title Insurance	Usually one of the larger fees you will pay as part of the transaction, title insurance is a policy that guarantees to the lender that you, in fact, own your property and no one else can claim a lien against it.
Government Recording Fee	Each county has their own records and their own fees.

What if my Spouse is Younger than 62?

The reverse mortgage is a program specifically for people aged 62 or older. What happens if one partner is 62 and the other is younger? Can you still get a reverse mortgage?

Yes. As long as one of the owners is over the age of 62, the couple can apply for a reverse mortgage. However, your ability to borrow equity will be greatly reduced. Usually it's better to wait until all owners of the home are over the age of 62.

But, if you want to continue and one spouse is under 62, special rules apply. The spouse under the age if 62 is considered a non-borrowing spouse. What does that mean? A non-borrowing spouse is someone who may be on title to the home but is not a borrower on the loan and therefore, is not responsible for the mortgage.

In the past, if the spouse who owned the house passed away, the non-borrowing spouse (married to someone who owns a home and not on the mortgage loan) was in trouble. What I mean is, the non-borrowing spouse would be out-ofcompliance with the reverse mortgage and thus would have to either move out and sell or refinance the loan.

However, the department of Housing and Urban Development (HUD) changed the rules in 2014 to allow a non-borrowing spouse a *deferral period*, which allows him or her to remain in the home.

A non-borrowing spouse is considered **qualified** to remain in the home after the borrower passes away, **as long as they were married at the time of the loan application and the spouse obliges to keep the home insured, taxes paid, and continues use the home as a primary residence.**

The loan will go into a deferral period, which is simply a nice way of saying that the lender will not try to collect on the mortgage. At the same time, access to additional funds on the credit line will likely be stopped. The lender will want to know the following:

- ✓ Was the non-borrowing spouse married to the borrower at the time of the loan closing? Did they remain married at the time the borrower passed away?
- ✓ Was the non-borrowing spouse listed as a non-borrowing spouse in the loan documents?
- ✓ Can the non-borrowing spouse prove that he or she has a legal right to live in the house, within 90 days of the borrower passing away?
- ✓ Does the non-borrowing spouse intend use the home as a primary residence?
- ✓ Are all other requirements of the loan being met?

I highly recommend speaking with an attorney if you find yourself in a situation where a non-borrowing spouse may be involved.

How do I Access My Cash?

Accessing cash depends on which reverse mortgage program you decide to go with.

With a reverse mortgage, the way you draw depends on the way you structured the loan. On a reverse mortgage with a <u>fixed interest rate</u>, you only get a one-time draw at closing, which means you get your cash when the mortgage is signed and funded. Usually there is a three-business day waiting period called the right of rescission.

The *right of rescission* period is mandated **on all mortgage refinance loans** (adjustable and fixed). The three-day waiting period exists in case you change your mind and decide not to go forward with a mortgage loan. If you choose to rescind (cancelling with no cost to you), you must notify the lender and/or the closing agent within those three days. After the three day wait period is over, your money is disbursed to you.

On an adjustable rate mortgage, you figure out (with the lender) how much you get at that time of closing. (Usually up to 40% of your available funds, less paying off any existing liens and mandatory obligations and fees.) Keep in mind, the right of rescission is still in effect, and does not include Sundays or federal holidays, so it is usually on the fourth day, when you will receive your money.

Then, if you have a line of credit, a greater amount (the remaining 60%) will be available after one year and one day.

If you choose not to advance the line of credit, the lender will make you aware at the time of closing, how you can access your money. Usually, it is attached to a document you send into the lender to notify them you wish to draw on your funds.

What are Term or Tenure Payments?

Depending on how much equity is available to you, there is an option available where you receive term or tenure payments.

These are only currently available with an adjustable rate mortgage. A term payment is one in which the client arranges with the lender to receive a certain amount of money every month for a fixed period. If that is the case, you need to provide a voided check at closing and the lender will set it up, so your money is deposited monthly into your account for the length of the term. A tenure payment is one in which the choice to make payments continues for the rest of your life.

Why is There a Line of Credit?

As you get deeper into the process of applying for a reverse mortgage, one of the critical questions you should be asking yourself is whether you want to consider a line of credit.

As previously stated, a line of credit option is only available on an adjustable-rate reverse mortgage. In order to qualify for a line of credit, you will also need to have substantial equity in your home. Usually this means you need to owe less than 40% of the appraised value. If you fall into that category, should you consider a line of credit?

Most people tend to lean toward the fixed-rate option because they are contemplating what the payments will be. Fixing the payments owed on a mortgage is a classic, consistent, and conservative way to go. The reverse mortgage is the exception.

With a reverse mortgage, having an adjustable-rate mortgage means you have the option of an additional line of credit. Look at it as a home equity line of credit that does not have monthly repayments. Assuming you have enough equity in your home, the lender will offer you a line of credit, which is usually the remaining available equity you can borrow on your home. Usually 40% of what you can borrow is available to you at the time of closing and the remaining 60% after one year and one day.

It is similar to having a credit card except you are not required to pay anything back during your lifetime. With the reverse mortgage line of credit, it grows through time, on average, 5% per year. That amount may not sound like much, but given time, the growth can be substantial.

How Quickly Can I Access my Money?

You have access to your cash in days. If you found yourself in need of immediate cash, you would normally go to a bank, who would likely suggest a home equity line of credit. The problem is that you would have to qualify for the line of credit and would be required to pay back the amount. You could also draw out of your savings, but then your savings stops working for you, as you would earn less interest. The same is true of a pension, stocks, or retirement accounts. You should consider what the full cost really is, when withdrawing money.

The reverse mortgage line of credit is usually accessible within a few days. You fill out a form, send it to the lender, and the money is wired to your account.

What most people do not know, is that you can also pay back the line of credit if you choose. Why would anyone want to do that? Isn't the main point of a reverse mortgage that you do not have to pay money back? Correct. However, the line of credit is usually flexible, meaning you can borrow and pay it back as much as you want. Paying back the line of credit means that you create availability again. You can keep using it as a cash flow tool when you need it, pay it off when you are in a better position to do so, or simply do nothing. It is up to the individual.

Is it a Taxed Income?

You do not owe taxes or have to pay any kind of tax on the money you access. Simply put, it is your money. The IRS considers a reverse mortgage a pledged asset, not an asset. This means it is not taxable. A pledged asset cannot be willed to someone. You CAN draw the money out of your line of credit if you wanted to give it to someone, but you cannot pass on the line of credit to someone after you pass away.

Is the Line of Credit Secure?

Prior to 2017, during a rough patch of unemployment, my friends Chris and Marina went out and got a HELOC (Home Equity Line of Credit) second mortgage.

Usually these were in the neighborhood of $50,000 or $100,000. They thought that if everything went wrong, at least the money would be there, for them to live on, until they got back on their feet.

Sounded great, but unfortunately, it was a very poor decision. Remember, this was 2007, during that time, banks started to get worried about who would pay them back and who would not. As a result, they cancelled the lines of credit, sometimes without even telling the borrowers. When clients would show up to access their lines of credit, they were shocked to learn it was NOT there.

This CANNOT happen with your line of credit because of the changes in 2017. The government stepped, in changed the rules, and improved them for consumers. One of the biggest changes was to protect consumers who had reverse mortgage lines of credit. **Even if your property value goes down, your line of credit cannot be cancelled as long as you keep paying your taxes and insurance and live in the home as your primary residence.** Read that again.

Can My Line of Credit Grow?

Your line of credit actually grows through time. At the time you make a loan application for a reverse mortgage, one of the documents is an amortization schedule. This schedule shows you what the predicted rate of growth will be on your line of credit. This is a standard disclosure when initially meeting with a loan officer to talk about a reverse mortgage.

As long as you do not draw every dime out, it will grow. Obviously, the more is unused, the faster the line of credit will grow. The growth rate is usually calculated at the current interest rate plus one-half percent per year.

You can make payments to the line of credit, paying off the interest, then the principal. When the principal drops, your line of credit will increase. In doing this, you would have access to that line of credit later.

Can the Line of Credit Exceed the Home's Value?

Though it is not likely to happen, the simple answer is yes. Remember in the 1980's when interest rates rose dramatically? What if you have a reverse mortgage with a line of credit and the same thing that happened in the 80's happens again? Suddenly, interest rates rise. At the same time, your line of credit will rise at the interest rate plus half a percentage point. What if interest rates shot up to 13.5%? Your line of credit would increase by 14% the next year. (13.5 + 0.5)

However, it is unlikely that your home would ever go that high. Most loans have a 5% cap on the adjustable rate, meaning that if you start at 4% and interest rates went to 10%, your rate would stop at the cap, which is 5% above where you started. In other words, your rate would be 9% (4% + 5%).

The line of credit cannot grow to more than 150% of the value of the home. If you found yourself in that situation, the line would simply stop growing once it reached that amount.

What Happens After I Pass Away?

One of the biggest misconceptions about reverse mortgages comes from what happens after the last borrower passes away.

Understanding what happens after you pass away is key to giving you the peace of mind that a reverse mortgage decision is right for you.

- ✓ The lender does not own your home when you pass away!
- ✓ The reverse mortgage loan is only payable when the last person on the loan leaves the home.
- ✓ If there is a couple, the loan is only due and payable when the last member of the couple passes away.

What Happens to My Home After I Pass Away?

When the last borrower passes away, the home will likely be part of an estate. Before you pass away, you will want to consult with a lawyer and, at the very least, draw up a will. I recommend an estate attorney because most people have more than just a few items they want to pass on.

You still own your home and it is not going to become the property of the bank after you pass away. Your home is part of your estate and does not belong to the bank, so what happens to the house depends on your wishes, not the lender's.

Assuming you have a will or estate plan, the home becomes part of the estate to be settled, usually by the attorney. The attorney will notify the lender that you have passed away. Once that occurs, the estate now has six months to settle everything before the mortgage is due and payable on the house.

Note: If six months isn't enough time, the estate or heirs can apply for two additional extensions of three months each, before the loan has to be settled. In other words, your heirs/estate do not have to make or settle the payment for six to twelve months after you pass away. However, the taxes, insurance, utilities need to be paid.

This is in contrast to what happens if you have a traditional mortgage on your home at the time you pass away. If you were to pass away at the end of a month, it is possible that heirs would be too grief-stricken to remember to make your mortgage payment. Next thing they know, they are in trouble. With a reverse mortgage, it is truly beneficial to have that extra time to get the mortgage settlement figured out.

After you pass away and your heirs have a chance to grieve, it is time to get down to business on what to do with your home and your reverse mortgage. Let's look at a couple of scenarios your heirs may face.

Scenario 1: You owe more than the home is worth.

This possibility scares people the most. The last thing anyone wants to do is leave his or her heirs in debt.

Say the home is worth $100,000 but the reverse mortgage is $125,000. In this situation, details are clearly defined in the documents signed when taking out a reverse mortgage to start with. Because it is a non-recourse loan, your heirs can <u>never</u> owe more than your home is worth. It also means that your home (not you/your estate) borrowed money. Therefore, the estate and the heirs are not responsible for paying the lender back more than the home is worth.

In the above scenario, your heirs or estate would have a decision to make. They have the option to purchase the home and pay off the lender for 95% of what the home appraises for or what is owed, whichever is less.

If the home appraised for $100,000 and the reverse mortgage was $125,000, the heirs could pay off the mortgage and own the home free and clear for $95,000. That is 95% of the value the appraised value. What happens to the remaining $35,000? FHA pays the lender the difference. That's how a non-recourse loan works. Cool huh?

Scenario 2: You owe less than the house is worth.

This happens most frequently. Using the same number in scenario 1, say the home is worth $100,000 and at the time you pass away, the reverse mortgage balance is $50,000.

Once your heirs notify the lender you have passed, the clock starts on the initial six-month period. The heirs do not need to make payments, but they do need to make decisions. Remember, they do have two additional three-month extensions available to them if they so choose. There is potential equity of $50,000 left in the home (amount the home is worth less the amount due to pay off the reverse mortgage). Whoever eventually takes ownership of the home will need to pay off the reverse mortgage, just as one would pay off any existing mortgage on a home that is an inheritance. He or she can choose to pay off the home and keep it to live in or rent. He or she could also sell the home, pay off what is owed and keep the profit. Heirs have choices.

Can I Refinance a Reverse Mortgage?

The simple answer is yes. Reverse mortgages do not have prepayment penalties, which means there is no financial penalty if you want to refinance. As with traditional mortgages, it can be refinanced to see if you can get better terms. However, there is a difference between refinancing a reverse mortgage and refinancing a traditional mortgage.

Most of the time, when people think of refinancing, they want to get cash to pay bills, lower payments or get a lower rate. With the reverse mortgage, it's not quite the same.

- ✓ You can refinance a reverse mortgage to change the terms of your loan.
- ✓ You can refinance a reverse mortgage to see if you can get more cash out.

The biggest factor is your home's worth. If you do not have enough equity in your home to refinance a reverse, it is not worth shopping around. Almost all reverse mortgage lenders have the same lending guidelines.

People who obtained a reverse mortgage prior to October 2, 2017, might have been able to get more money out than now. If you have a reverse mortgage from that time, it is worth finding out if you can refinance, depending on the value of your home.

Continually refinancing your reverse mortgage is not a good idea. You will have to pay fees all over again, which will eat away at your equity.

Back in the 90's, one of the big legal scams occurred when people would 'churn and burn' their mortgage. This was aided by what I can only call *unscrupulous mortgage brokers/lenders*. Unscrupulous mortgage lenders would fund a loan for you and then a year later, call you to see if you were in debt again, and sell you a new mortgage (usually at a higher rate and more fees).

In the reverse mortgage world, this cannot happen anymore. To be able to refinance an existing reverse mortgage, you have to see a benefit of five times the cost of the loan. That means if the loan costs $5,000, you need to see a benefit of at least $25,000 or the lender cannot do it.

This is protectionary. The other rule is that at least five percent of the new loan amount must be available to you in cash. For example, if you have a new loan for $200,000, the loan will have to make at least 5% available to you in cash ($10,000) or the loan cannot be completed. All this prevents the *unscrupulous* behavior that was common in the 1990's.

What if my Home Needs Repairs?

It depends on how extensive the repairs are and what you owe on your home. Generally, if your home has structural defects, like the foundation is caving in or something is structurally wrong with the home, you are going to need to fix it, prior to completing a reverse mortgage. If your home is a safety or health hazard, it would need to be fixed before obtaining a reverse mortgage.

Can I Buy a Home with a Reverse Mortgage?

Amazingly, I do not get this question as much as I thought I would. The simple answer is, yes! Buying a home with a reverse mortgage is something relatively new and not many people realize it is possible. In the past, you had to first, buy the home for cash or financing. Then, you had to wait awhile before refinancing into a reverse mortgage.

Here is an example: Say you (age 62+) have a $300,000 home you own free and clear. You sell it yourself and pay all the costs, so you can preserve what you have from the sale. With $300,000 in the bank, you decide to buy a new home with a reverse mortgage. You could always just buy a $300,000 home in cash. You would have no mortgage payments. However, you would also have no cash left. A reverse mortgage is different. It will allow you to either buy more or put down less.

That is right! You can buy more or put down less. This is how it work. Instead of paying cash for the property, instead, use a reverse mortgage to buy the home. You can put down $183,000 and finance $117,000. The immediate advantage would be that instead of putting all your money into your home, you would be able to keep $117,000 in the bank for whatever you wanted. If the home needs repairs, spend some money to make it yours! Here are some estimates:

	Paying Cash	Reverse Mortgage*
*Down Payment	$300,000	$183,000
*Cash Remaining	$0	$117,000
*Mortgage Payment	$0	$0

*These are estimates.

What if you want to buy a bigger home? This is quite common. What if you move to a new town and thought you could buy a home for $300,000 yet find out what you <u>like</u> and what you can <u>afford</u> were two different realities. What happens if you are on a fixed income, do not want to make mortgage payments, or would not qualify for a mortgage. Does that mean you are out of luck? **Nope!**

Let's use the same $300,000 example of buying a home. You have looked at everything available and have decided that you really need to spend $500,000 to get the home you want. You have $300,000 cash, and maybe another $25,000 you could dip into if needed, but that simply is NOT enough money. You could use a reverse mortgage to 'downsize by upsizing.'

	Paying Cash	Reverse Mortgage*
Purchase Price	$500,000	$500,000
Down Payment	$300,000	$300,684
Reverse Mortgage	$0	$199,316
Additional Required	$200,000	$0

*These are estimates.

If you paid cash, you would need to qualify for a mortgage. Your payments would be around $1,200 a month, if you qualified. It also means you need to show proof of making at least $3,600 a month and gets even more complicated from there.

With a reverse mortgage, there are no mortgage payments for the rest of your life as long as you live in the home, pay property taxes, keep it insured, and maintain the property. Your $300,000 gives you options.

Why Isn't Everyone Doing This?

My answer is always the same. Most people do not know about the option. Even most Realtors do not know this is an option! (Share this book with them.)

What are the Requirements?

The requirements to use a reverse mortgage for purchasing a home are similar to the requirements of financing an existing home.

1. You must plan to occupy the home as a primary residence, at least six months and one day a year.

2. Only your primary residence can take advantage a reverse mortgage. You cannot use a reverse mortgage on a vacation home or a second property. However, you could get money out of your primary residence to buy a vacation home or second property.
3. Have a fully executed sales contract to purchase the new home. Again, this is standard when purchasing a home, regardless of financing.
4. Complete HECM counseling. (This is the golden ticket I mentioned earlier in the book.) HECM counseling should be done before looking at homes. The counselor is going to ask you for your address, and you want to be able to relay your current address.
5. Complete a financial assessment with the lender. The purpose of the financial assessment is to prove that you can afford to pay the taxes and insurance on your new home and still have money left to live on. It is also to ensure you can afford the upkeep and maintenance.

What do I Provide to my Loan Officer?

Documents needed from the borrower at the time of application:

- ✓ Copy of HECM Counseling Certificate – Signed by the counselor, all borrowers, and non-borrowing spouses

- ✓ A copy of <u>one</u> of the following for each borrower and co-borrower:
    - o Driver's License, or
    - o State-issued Id card, or
    - o Passport, or
    - o Birth Certificate

- ✓ A copy of ONE of the following for each borrower and eligible, non-borrowing spouse.
    - o Social Security Card, or
    - o Medicare Card, or
    - o W2, or
    - o Social Security Awards Letter or statement

- ✓ Homeowner's Insurance Agent Name and Number
    - o If you have found a home to purchase and have provided your agent with this information, they can provide an estimate of your insurance costs.

- ✓ Property Tax Bill
    - o Usually the Realtor or title company can provide this.

- ✓ Most Recent Mortgage Statement for ALL mortgages you currently have.
    - o This includes HELOC's (Home Equity Lines of Credit), First Mortgages, or any other liens

- ✓ Copy of any Living Trusts.
    - o Copies must be signed and notarized versions of the ENTIRE trust and any/all amendments or restatements

- ✓ Original Power of Attorney, it applicable.

- ✓ Alternative Contact – Name, address, and phone number of a friend or relative to keep on file

- ✓ Income, Asset, and Expenses:
  - o Income if employed:
    - ▪ Last 30 days Paystubs
    - ▪ W2s for the past two years
  - o Income from Social Security & Pension
    - ▪ 1099s for the past 2 years
    - ▪ Federal tax returns for past 2 years
  - o Assets:
    - ▪ Bank statements and/or investment account statements, all pages for the last two months
  - o Expenses:
    - ▪ Social security numbers to pull credit report for mortgages and verification of payments

- ✓ Depending on the lender, a credit card number for the home to be appraised.

Who is the Perfect Candidate for a Reverse Mortgage?

The perfect candidate for a reverse mortgage is an older homeowner. Anyone who can benefit from better cash flow every month has the potential to be a candidate for a reverse mortgage.

I had a 63-year-old client named Shelly. She had social security income, but nothing else. She paid off her home but was having problems because she was not making enough from social security to live on. She was worried she couldn't afford the home unless she got some help, went back to work, or sold the home. Clearly, she could sell the home, but it would not have solved the issue of where she would live the rest of her life. Shelly was in the situation where she was 'house rich, cash poor.'

A reverse mortgage was a perfect solution for her because she asked that a LESA account be set up. As earlier discussed, with a LESA or Life Expectancy Set Aside, a portion of her equity would be set aside to pay property taxes and insurance for the rest of her life expectancy.

By using her equity to cover taxes and insurance on the home, she could focus on if or when she wanted to work and alleviated the pressure of having to save for tax and insurance payments. For someone who was used to operating on a fixed income, Shelly's whole world changed.

I met a gentleman named Brian who had medical issues. As a result, he could not get conventional health insurance. He took out a reverse mortgage with a line of credit, so if he ever needed it, he could tap the line of credit to help cover future medical expenses. A reverse mortgage is a phenomenal financial-planning tool that allows you to free up cash flow and have more choices.

I had the pleasure of working with a couple who funded their retirement by moving into a fourplex. Bill and Robyn decided to sell their large, suburban home, and had $500,000. However, they had very little savings and they needed a place to live. They decided to buy a home with four units. The paid cash, renovated the first unit for themselves, renovated the other three units to rent, charging $1,000 a month per unit. After their friends moved in, they refinanced with a reverse mortgage. Because they were living in one of the units, they qualified. No more monthly mortgage payments! They significantly reduced their cost-of-living and as a result, were able to fund their retirement.

Are my Government Benefits Affected?

Check with a Federal Benefits Administrator (the government). That being said, the answer is usually *no*.

Reverse mortgages are not considered income. Therefore, they do not affect government benefits like social security. The one exception is Medicaid, where you are means-tested. However, people on Medicaid usually do not own houses or have assets.

Do I Need to Have my Home Paid Off?

No. For example, if your home is worth $100,000, you want to owe less than $50,000. This is protectionary for both you and the lender. Prior to 2017, you could borrow a lot more, but lenders were lending too much. If a borrower wanted to sell, he or she was not left with enough equity to get out of a property without paying. Hence, the new rules were put into place.

To figure out if a reverse mortgage is an option, start by calculating your home's worth. (There are several websites designed to give property values.) Divide the number in half and compare it to what you owe. If you owe less than half, you should have the equity necessary to complete a reverse mortgage.

Am I Selling my House to the Bank?

The simple answer is *no*. This is a common misconception. You are not selling or surrendering your home to a bank if you take out a reverse mortgage. It is simply not how the process works. What you ARE doing, is taking advantage of a specific loan program developed especially for seniors. There is no mystery to it. Seniors are a good credit risk for lenders, as they usually have steady sources of income. It is a win-win for both client and lender.

What Happens to my Equity?

Your equity is going to allow you to stay in your home without having to make mortgage payments. The equity is defined as what the home is worth, less what you owe. If your home is worth $100,000 and you owe $50,000, you have $50,000 in equity. When you take out a reverse mortgage, you are allowing the reverse mortgage lender to refinance the $50,000 you owe, plus fees and costs. After everything is said and done and the mortgage is $60,000, it means you have equity worth $40,000. Usually the value of your home will increase. After a couple years, your home may be worth $110,000. Your mortgage will accrue interest. Let's say the interest you accrued is $4,000. You may owe $64,000, but your home has also increased in value. Now, you have $46,000 in equity

The reverse mortgage program is designed to make sure you maintain an equity position in your home through time. If you chose to move or sell, you would have to pay off the mortgage balance, just like any other mortgage loan. The program is designed to preserve your equity.

Can I Pay More Than Required?

All reverse mortgages can be paid down or paid off without penalty. You can make payments to the balance at any time, without penalty. It is a government regulation/requirement. If you select a line of credit option, making payments to your mortgage may free up more money on your line of credit. Ask your specific lender whether that is the case. It usually is.

Is it Better to Wait or Jump Now?

I suggest getting a reverse mortgage as soon as you qualify. As witnessed in 2017, protocols drastically changed. I argue they were for the better because the changes largely helped consumers, but it drove a lot of lenders out of the industry.

Programs change. If you like what you are hearing, I would jump now. If you are looking at the line of credit option on a reverse mortgage, the answer is definitely NOW. In addition to freeing up your cash flow, the line of credit will grow through time. The sooner you get it, the bigger the line of credit can grow.

SECTION 12: RED FLAG LOOK-OUTS

The Right of Rescission

The Right of Rescission is a period between signing loan documents and a fully funded loan. It is a federally-mandated requirement of all refinances, whether a traditional or reverse mortgage. The day you sign your mortgage papers does not count towards the right of rescission. At closing, you are given a couple of documents to sign. Usually there are three copies of the Right of Rescission. This is a *get out of jail free* card if you decide not to move forward with the mortgage transaction. Hopefully, the person conducting your closing will give you the Right of Rescission paperwork and inform you that if you change your mind, all you have to do is sign the right of rescission and return it to the lender or title company before the three day period is up. That cancels everything. The lender must cancel the file, refund any money you paid to them, and cannot charge you for the appraisal. (The lender does not have to give you the appraisal either.) You have three business days to change your mind. Sundays and national holidays do not count.

Higher interest rates are not always bad.

When it comes to traditional mortgages, everyone is trying to negotiate the lowest, possible rate. A reverse mortgage is a little bit different. A higher interest rate on a reverse mortgage means a line of credit will grow faster. Most reverse mortgages fall into this category.

The line of credit grows through time. As your home becomes more valuable, you should be able to access the equity. As your home increases in value, so does your line of credit. However, the higher the interest rate on the loan, the faster the line of credit will grow. Remember, on a traditional mortgage, the interest rate determines the payment. On a reverse mortgage, there are no required payments, so the interest rate is not as important. As a result, reverse mortgage interest rates do not tend to fluctuate the way forward rates do.

Start the reverse mortgage at 61½-years-old.
You probably have not thought about half-birthdays since you were a kid. Nevertheless, half-birthdays actually mean something now. I would not recommend starting until maybe a month or so before your 62nd birthday. Reason being, if you apply for counseling, the certificate is only good for six months. Plan accordingly; because you do not want to take the reverse mortgage, counseling only to find out it expired before you had a chance to complete the transaction. However, you technically can start applying when you are 61½ plus one day.

You are not required to buy anything else.
A reverse mortgage does not require you to buy anything else as part of the transaction. Chances are that you already have an insurance agent, financial planner, and/or accountant.

There is no reason for you to have to change vendors in order get your mortgage completed. You do not have to take out a special insurance policy or have your taxes done by someone. There are no other requirements that you buy anything in order to complete the mortgage.

Years ago, there used to be something called credit life and disability. It was insurance offered by the lender, in case something happened to you and could not make your payments. The sales pitch was that it was just a "little bit of money, up front" as part of your payments and then if something happens, are covered. This does not usually happen anymore. However, if for some reason someone is telling you that have to make a purchase as part of the transaction, do not work with him or her. Instead, find someone who is 100% authentic.

A second appraisal may be required.

Part of the reverse mortgage process is that the U.S. Department of Housing and Urban Development must review all appraisals before reverse mortgage files can be completed. This is standard as part of the reverse mortgage process. It usually happens out-of-view, meaning the response from HUD is a NO and there is no second appraisal required. However, sometimes, a file gets randomly selected for an audit and a second appraisal is required. If that happens, it simply means the file may take an extra week to close because another appraiser is sent out, requiring a second report.

SECTION 13: PREPARING FOR AN APPRAISAL

Here are some tips to help you ensure that the experience with appraisal goes as smoothly as possible. The first aspect to recognize about an appraisal is that it is a snapshot of your home at that time. <u>It does not reflect what you are going to sell your home for, nor does it signify the price you can sell your home</u>. An appraisal does not determine the highest value obtainable. It protects the lender and confirms there is <u>value</u> in the home. Oftentimes, when speaking with a Realtor, you are offered a different value than an appraiser does. This happens because a Realtor is usually hyper-aware of the market. They know when homes go up for sale and when others sell.

Realtors are more aware of the market than appraisers are because Realtors and appraisers have two different end-goals in mind. The Realtor is motivated to sell your home for the highest possible amount. An appraiser is there to protect the lender and will be much more conservative in their evaluation. Neither one is incorrect; they simply have different objectives. Ultimately, the appraisal value of your home determines how much money you can acquire with a reverse mortgage.

The $275 Mistake with a $15 Fix:

Most reverse mortgage transactions require an FHA appraisal. FHA (Federal Housing Authority) is the body that governs reverse mortgages. They have some unusual rules around homes and appraisals. The *$275 Mistake* is not having a carbon monoxide detector plugged in within 15 feet of all bedrooms. Detectors can be purchased in almost any home-improvement store for around $15. This is crucial. Here is an example of why...

I had a client named Mike who did not have a carbon monoxide detector, which the FHA appraiser was nice enough to point out to him. A week later, a notice arrived which revealed the FHA appraiser's findings and even though Mike dutifully went and bought a detector the following day, he would be charged $275 to return for re-inspection. The $275 charge would have been for (maybe) ten minutes of work. Don't make the same mistake as Mike. Spend the $15 to solve the issue before it becomes a problem.

Fix What Needs to be Fixed First:

Again, FHA has a different set of rules. When it comes to FHA appraisals, I tell clients to repair whatever possible, before the appraiser arrives. From a cracked window to a leaky faucet, if something is broken, fix it. Remember appraisers are looking for what is wrong, as much as what is right.

If you have made upgrades to your home, make sure you communicate those to the appraiser.

Clean, Clean, Clean:

When it comes to getting your home appraised, clean, clean, clean your home. Technically, it does not matter if your home is clean or not because the appraiser should not be looking at your housecleaning skills to evaluate the value of your home. However, I have found that if your home is clean, the appraiser seems more willing to overlook other small items. It is all perspective and the cleanliness factor creates an impression that you care about the home.

The Appraised Value Always Comes in Low:

I had a prospective client who had an appraisal done prior to meeting with me. He had been working with a previous lender and did not like what he was hearing, so he called me. In a nutshell, he felt the appraisal had come in too low and after reading, I agreed with him. Regardless, an FHA appraisal is tied to the home for at least four months. Once it occurs, you cannot have a new appraisal executed for at least four months. As I explained to the prospective client, there nothing to do about it. It is just how it works with FHA.

Can you appeal the appraised value? The short answer is *yes*, but it is most likely you will lose. It is not worth the hassle. I have <u>never</u> won an FHA appraisal appeal in twenty-five years of business. **<u>Never</u>**. Can you fight an appraisal? Yes. Should you? No. Wait four months and try again.

SECTION 14: STEP-BY-STEP GUIDANCE

Congratulations on deciding to take the next step and initiate a reverse mortgage. The following section breaks down the steps of the reverse mortgage process in a simple-to-read format.

1. Meet with a Loan Officer

Meet with someone you feel comfortable with, but also someone who is knowledgeable about how the reverse mortgage process works. <u>Not all loan officers are trained equally</u>. I am constantly amazed by people who relay stories about previous experiences with loan officers. <u>If someone does not sound knowledgeable, choose someone else. It is your money and your future!</u> You deserve someone who understands how to get you exactly what you want.

2. Discuss your Options

When I do proposals, I will run a couple of scenarios by the client, which may fit needs. It is a get-to-know-you session that allows the lender and the client to both get on the same page.

3. FHA/HUD Counseling

This process is nowhere near as intimidating as it sounds. The purpose of FHA/HUD counseling is two-fold. First, it ensures you understand what you are doing. It also ensures you haven't been coerced or pressured by the loan officer, lending company, family member, or anyone. It is also there to determine whether you are lucid enough to get reverse mortgage and understand what you are doing.

Once the counseling is completed, I ask my clients to request that the FHA/HUD Counselor email a copy of their completion certificate to me. I do this because the counseling certificate is the golden ticket to getting a reverse mortgage completed. Usually, a loan officer won't even take a loan application if the counseling hasn't been completed.

4. Sign the Application

Once you have completed the counseling, it is time to meet with the loan officer again. This time, to sign a mountain of paperwork. This is also where the loan officer collects copies of your paperwork. You will also be asked to sign a document called the *Intent To Proceed* or ITP document. This lets the lender know you want to proceed with the loan process. Because this is such a large transaction and no one knows how long the loan will last, there is a lot of paper.

5. Your File is Sent to Processing

Once all documents are collected and signatures verified, the loan officer prepares your documents and sends them to the lender for processing. From the customer's perspective, there really is not much to this part. Your loan is assigned to a processor, the documents are sorted, and the appraisal is ordered.

6. The Appraisal

Appraisers are like lawyers, inspectors, and dentists. Their job is to look at what is wrong. If you have something wrong with your home, it is best to discuss it with your loan officer first. You are required to arrange payment for the appraisal at the time of service.

7. Processing and Underwriting

Once the appraisal is in, the processor will turn your file over to the underwriter, whose job is to verify all the information you provided. Occasionally, underwriters will ask for clarification. The underwriter may ask for specific items called conditions. Conditions are requirements that must be met in order for the loan to fund.

Once the underwriting team has reviewed the appraisal/documents and determined that everything looks good, they will issue a *clear to close* with final loan approval.

8. Closing

The closing team will take over and prepare the documents for signing at closing. Usually, this when the closing time and signing will be set up.

9. 3-Day Waiting Period

The *3-day-right-of-rescission-period* comes into play. It starts at midnight the day after you close. Remember, the three days do not include Sundays or national holidays. On the fourth day, the loan funds.

Section 15: After Closing

Most people do not give much thought as to what happens after their loan is complete. With a reverse mortgage, there are a few concepts you need to be aware of after closing.

Drawing funds:

If you requested funds be made available to you at closing, they are now available. You may ask for funds to be deposited into your account or paid with a cashier's check. You will want to clarify your choice at closing.

The Occupancy Certificate:

There is one very important requirement called the yearly occupancy statement. The occupancy statement is mailed to you once a year and you are required to fill it out and verify you still live in your home as the primary residence. If you do not fill out and return the document, the lender can decide that you do not actually live in the home and call the note, which is a fancy way of saying the lender contacts you to let you know that you violated the terms of the loan. Then you would have to pay the borrowed money, or your loan could go into default and eventually foreclosure.

Monthly Statements:

Even though you do not have a monthly mortgage payment anymore, the lender will usually send you a monthly statement of your account. If you have a line of credit, this is where you will find what is available.

Servicing:

If you have had a traditional mortgage in the past, chances are you received a notice stating that a new lender is servicing your loan. If you get a notice that your servicing has changed, it means your loan has been sold to another company. This happens quite frequently and does not really affect you at all. I recommend keeping the most recent mortgage statement in a file with your important papers, like your will and/or your estate plan.

Heirs:

Although it may be uncomfortable to think about, and even more awkward to discuss, there are some tips for making life easier for your heirs once the last borrower leaves the home.

✓ Authorizing an Heir: Early on, it is best to contact the lender and authorize an heir on your loan. Setting up an authorization is as easy as calling the 800 number on your monthly statement and asking the lender for written authorization to communicate with your heirs. There are incredible restrictions when it comes to financial privacy. As a result, providing authorization will allow your heirs to talk to the lender and communicate about the mortgage, after you have left the home. This truly saves your heirs headaches down the road. Without your permission, the lender cannot talk to your heirs about your mortgage or home. Providing authorization helps speed up the process.

✓ Keep a file: It is wise to create a file with all your reverse mortgage paperwork in. You can file your monthly statements there and clearly marking it as *reverse mortgage* will help your heirs in the future.

Heir's responsibilities:

The first job of the heirs is to get in contact with the lender and let him or her know that the borrowers have either left the home or passed away. Again, this is where an authorization will help. If there is not an authorization on file, the mortgage company will insist on lawyers getting involved and wait for an administrator to be named.

Keep in mind, interest will continue to accrue on the loan. Remember, your heirs have an initial six-month period to settle the reverse mortgage account and if for some reason need more time, can always apply for two additional three-month extensions.

Next, the heirs will need to have the title to the home changed to their name/names. Usually this involves an attorney, title company, or both. The lender is also involved because there are some decisions made as to what happens to the home.

Much depends on what the heirs want to do with the home.

If heirs want to sell the home:

First, heirs need to establish their right to sell the home. If there is not an attorney handling the estate, it may be worth spending a little money to converse with one about how you can establish ownership of the property.

An attorney will be able to help heirs sort through the requirements of legally changing ownership of the home. It is also a good idea to inform the lender of your intent, as he or she will need to provide a payoff statement at some point. It is required that the reverse mortgage be paid off during the sale. Like a traditional mortgage, the home is appraised. Then, the title company will use the appraised value and subtract the payoff balance provided by the lender. The remaining balance of funds is what goes to heirs.

If heirs want to keep the home:

Heirs will need to pay off the reverse mortgage or refinance it into a new first mortgage. This can be accomplished by either paying off the loan with cash, refinancing the home into a traditional first mortgages, or refinancing it as another reverse mortgage (if they intend to live there and meet the lending requirements).

Earlier, I covered the concept of a non-recourse loan. This is where it comes into play. Usually, heirs inherit equity. This allows them to sell the home, pay off the mortgage, and still see a profit. When **the loan is higher than the appraised value,** it is referred to as being *underwater* or *upside-down*. Since a reverse mortgage is a non-recourse loan, heirs still have options. They can choose to buy the home from the lender for 95% of the lesser of the balance owed or the appraised value. For example, a home is worth $100,000 but the mortgage is $125,000. Heirs could buy the home for $95,000 and the lender would petition FHA for reimbursement of the rest. The heirs cannot inherit debt, which is probably the best part about non-recourse loans.

Your heirs could elect <u>not</u> to purchase the home and it becomes the lender's issue. The house goes into foreclosure and the lender attempts to sell it to regain what is potentially lost.

Again, having the authorization granted, title cleared, and heirs ready to act quickly and knowledgably when needed, saves a lot of frustrated when the time comes. All the roadblocks can be removed in advance so heirs can make unhurried decisions, free from pressures of a looming foreclosure. The effects of advance planning can mean peace of mind and saving thousands of dollars in unnecessary fees due to delays and foreclosure actions.

Home Health Care:

Toward the end of my grandmother's life, the only thing she wanted to do was stay in the home she had lived in with my grandfather for the past forty years. At the time, I knew very little about this subject. Had I known then, what I know now, I would have insisted on the reverse mortgage path for her. A reverse mortgage can create cash flow in retirement. Another way to use a reverse mortgage is to fund in-home healthcare. After all, it is your home and your equity. Why not use it to improve your life?

Many people believe that medical insurance will cover in-home, long-term health care. However, most insurance plans do not cover it. Contrast that with statistics, on the Home Care Association of America website. In their findings, more than seventy percent of people over the age of sixty-five will need assistance at some point. Clearly there is a need but most importantly, there is a benefit to home health care. Studies have shown that *aging in place* has tremendous health and emotional benefits. Anyone who has spent time in a hospital or nursing home will likely admit aging in place at home is a much better option. A reverse mortgage can help you pay for in-home health care. This is much more than just another loan program. This is an opportunity to keep yourself in control of your life and health care.

- Most in home health care is paid for privately and not from insurance companies. (97%)

- The cost of in-home health care can run $40,000 to $50,000 a year; with 24/7, in-home health care costs that average $90,000 to $150,000 a year.

- Long Term Care Insurance, VA benefits, and Medicare will not cover 100% of in-home care services.

With reverse mortgages, seniors have the availability to tap into that equity to cover the difference between what in-home health care costs, and what insurance doesn't pay. The main reason a reverse mortgage is ideal for someone looking to fund in-home health care is that the process is relatively simple. Compared to other programs and options to pay for in-home health care, the reverse mortgage is pretty clear-cut.

A Reverse Mortgage is Better Than a HELOC Loan:

Usually, when I have the conversation about a reverse mortgage with seniors and/or their families, someone always brings up a home equity loan. Look at the differences.

Requirements	Home Equity Line of Credit	Reverse Mortgage
Equity in home	Yes	Yes
Credit Score Driven	Yes	No
Debt-to-Income	Yes	No
Monthly Payments	Yes	No
Can be bank frozen	Yes	No
Line of credit can increase	No	Yes
FHA Insured	No	Yes
Non-recourse feature	No	Yes
Specifically, for seniors	No	Yes

Whether looking for a home equity line of credit or a reverse mortgage, you must have some level of equity in your home. You must also have above a certain credit score in order to qualify for a loan.

With a home equity line of credit, there are credit score requirements. If your scores are too low, you will not qualify. With a reverse mortgage, there are no credit score requirements. A reverse mortgage is determined by age and available equity, not credit score.

The debt-to-income requirement is a nice way of asking whether you can afford to make payments, after you draw on your mortgage. If you are on a fixed income and money is running tight, borrowing money that requires a monthly repayment is not going to help in the long run. On the other hand, a reverse mortgage does not have this feature. You are never required to make monthly payments.

During the mortgage crisis of 2007 and 2008, one of the first problems was that banks were freezing home equity lines of credit to manage exposure to risk. The banks quickly realized they had large sums of money committed to home equity lines of credit, which meant they had exposure to loss they could not control or predict. Imagine being a homeowner during that time and you lost your job. You used to be able to tap the home equity line of credit, get some quick cash, and maybe ride things out until you were able to get a new job and/or pay off the line of credit. Imagine finding out the bank decided to freeze your account because they deemed you a risk! They were bleak times. With a reverse mortgage, lenders cannot do this. Once you take out your reverse mortgage, as long as you follow the few simple rules, the bank cannot freeze or shut it off.

A home equity line of credit almost never increases. If you wanted to increase your line of credit, you would have to requalify with new bank statements, new financial records, and a new appraisal, all of which cost money, time and there is no guarantee of approval. With a reverse mortgage, if you choose the line of credit option, your line of credit grows as your home continues to appreciate.

Most home equity lines of credit are considered second mortgages. What that means is when you get a home equity line of credit, you already have a mortgage in place. Your home equity line of credit is in *second position*, which means there is a larger fixed mortgage in front of it. As a result, most home equity lines of credit are not FHA insured whereas a reverse mortgage is.

One of the elements that makes a reverse mortgage so attractive is the FHA-insured product with a non-recourse feature. If you ever find yourself owing more than your home is worth, you do not have to make up the difference.

Let's say your home was worth $300,000 before 2008 and you owed $250,000 on it. That would mean $50,000 in equity. Then 2008 came, and all of a sudden home prices plummeted. The bank stepped in and said,

> *You owe $250,000 but your home is worth only $225,000. As a result, you need to pay your mortgage down by at least $25,000 or more, or we will foreclose.*

It got worse if you wanted to sell your home. At that point, if you sold, you would still owe money, even after the home sold. As a result, you would sell your home and still find yourself owing the bank money. A reverse mortgage protects you from this scenario with the non-recourse feature.

Finally, the reverse mortgage's biggest advantage is that it is specifically designed for seniors, whereas a home equity line of credit is not. If you are a senior who wants to age-in-place or needs help covering the cost of health care and you want to maintain your independence and lifestyle, a reverse mortgage is the answer.

Section 16: In Conclusion

Now that you have learned about what a reverse mortgage really is, I want to float an idea by you. Reverse mortgage has always had a negative connotation. Instead, let's call the reverse mortgage what it is, a retirement mortgage.

So, let's say that you are 62 and you are currently working. You've worked your whole life. You've been diligently paying your mortgage down. Now, at 62, you have some options and one of them is the 'retirement mortgage.'

You have a choice.

You can keep your existing mortgage in place. If you do that, let's say it's a 30-year mortgage. You have to pay it every month on the first. If you pay it past the 10th of the month, you have a late fee. If you don't pay it by the 30th, it effects your credit.

Then, let's say you pay it for the whole year, and in December, a tornado comes and rips the roof off your house, and you need to fix it. If you went to the lender and asked them to refund you money, so you could pay that, their response would be to laugh at you, and then decline to do it.

But, with a retirement mortgage (reverse mortgage), you could make payments on any day you want, or never at all. You could pay your mortgage as usual, and if you have a line of credit, you would be adding to that line every month.

Then, the same scenario happens, a tornado comes and rips off your roof. But because you have a retirement mortgage with a line of credit feature, you can go to the lender and ask for every cent you paid for the year back, and guess what? They would give it back to you.

No one would ever call you. No one would ever hound you for a payment or tell you, you are doing it wrong.

So, consider for a second that the 'retirement mortgage' does exist. It's called a reverse mortgage.

Reverse mortgages are not too good to be true; they are too good to be free.

Just think about this for a second. Imagine a loan program that would allow you to live in your home for the rest of your life, without mortgage payments. Imagine a loan program that would allow you to draw the equity in your home for any desired purpose.

It is time to start dreaming…

**A reverse mortgage
Isn't too good to be true.
It's too good to be free.**
-Jarred J. Talmadge

Adjustable rate

When the interest rate charged by the lender to the borrower can change.

Aging in place

When someone wants to get older but stay in their home, as opposed to being moved to a senior living or assisted living facility.

Amortization schedule

The schedule by which principal and interest rate paid back to the lender.

Appraisal

The appraisal is a professional evaluation of your property by an independent third party, to provide the lender with proof of value of your home at the time the loan was requested.

Closing costs

Closing costs are the price you pay to advance your loan to completion.

Deferral period

This is a period of time where the lender will continue to charge interest on the loan. The taxes and insurance must be paid to maintain the home, but the lender will take no action to otherwise collect the loan during this period

Doveryai no proberyai
It's Russian for 'trust' but verify' which was made famous by President Reagan in the 1980's when talking about dealing with people you don't 100% trust.

Equity
The amount of money left, by subtracting the mortgage balance and any other liens on a property, from the value of the home.

Escrow account
An escrow account is an account set up by the lender to pay your property taxes and insurance for you, when they are due.

FHA
Stands for Federal Housing Administration (or FHA), they are the government agency that oversees mortgage lending guidelines and insures loans against loss by lenders.

FHA counseling
All reverse mortgages required the borrowers and the non-borrowing spouses to take an FHA counseling course to make sure you are aware of what a reverse mortgage entails and to make sure you are lucid enough to accept a reverse mortgage.

Financial assessment	This is the means test that a lender must ask a client about, prior to engaging in a reverse mortgage. This must demonstrate a benefit to the borrower in order for the loan process to begin.
Good faith estimate	This is a document that outlines the expected fees and costs you might incur on a loan, prior to making the loan.
HECM	This is the acronym for Home Equity Conversion Mortgage, which is the legal name for a reverse mortgage.
HECM for purchase	This is the legal term for using a Home Equity Conversion Mortgage (a reverse mortgage) to purchase a new home
HELOC	Acronym for Home Equity Line of Credit. This is a line of credit with the house as collateral. Usually these loans are lines of credit secured by interest only payments or lower initial payments for the first ten years of the loan, then fully amortizing after the 10 year period.

HUD

This is the short term for Department of Housing and Urban Development. This is the government department that includes FHA, the Federal Housing Administration.

Interest rate

The interest rate is the rate that is charged to the borrower, by the lender, as the cost of borrowing money.

LESA

Stands for Life Expectancy Set Aside, which means an escrow account that has enough money set aside to pay your taxes and insurance for the rest of your life expectancy.

Life cap

The maximum percent that can be added to the starting interest rate, to determine the customer's interest rate. An adjustable rate cannot exceed the life cap, regardless of how high interest rates go.

Lock

The term refers to guaranteeing an interest rate for a set period of time.

Maintenance

Refers to keeping the home in acceptable condition for living in.

Mandatory obligations	These are obligations that must be paid in order for the loan to go forward. These could be things like the mortgage, or any lien on the house that must be paid before the loan is completed.
Mortgage insurance	This is a fee charged by FHA to the borrower. It is an insurance policy against the borrower defaulting on the loan, but it is also an insurance policy guaranteeing the borrower will never pass on debt to the heirs.
Non-Borrowing spouse	A non-borrowing spouse is someone who may be on title to the home but is not a borrower on the loan and therefore, is not responsible for the mortgage.
Non-recourse loan	A non-recourse loan means your home, not you, own the debt. Which means when you pass away, your heirs can never be forced to pay more than what is owed on the property they inherit, regardless of the situation.
Right of Rescission	This is the federally mandated three business day waiting period before your loan disburses to you on the

fourth business day. Sundays and federal holidays are not included as days of rescission.

Second position This refers to the mortgage position in terms of getting paid. A mortgage in second position would be paid off, after the first mortgage was paid. Also called a junior lien.

Tenure payments Tenure payments are payments that are made every month from your reverse mortgage for the rest of your life.

Term payments Term payments are payments that are made every month from your reverse mortgage, for a limited amount of time.

Traditional mortgage Refers to a forward mortgage, where the lender loans money to a borrower, in exchange for monthly payments every month for a set period of time.

Jarred Talmadge

Though reverse mortgages have been around since the 1980's. Until now, nobody has taken the time to lay out the benefits in a consumer-friendly format.

Internationally Published Author and Speaker, and Area Sales Manager Jarred Talmadge explains in simple, easy to understand ways, how a reverse mortgage can change your retirement for the better.

Whether thinking about a reverse mortgage or are in the field working as a Realtor, loan officer, or financial planner, this guide is for you.

If you are looking to work with Jarred, or you want to talk to him about speaking engagements, book sales or just talk reverse mortgage, you can contact Jarred:

Direct: 303-257-6246
Email: ThreeFeetPublishing2020@gmail.com

Or link to him on LinkedIn at:
www.linkedin.com/in/JarredTalmadge

LEGAL DISCLOSURES

This book is for informational purposes only. Any information shared within this book is understood to be true and accurate but are not verified in any way. The names have been changed to protect the identity of the clients mentioned.

Always do your own due diligence and use your own judgements when making a decision regarding your own home and your own finances. The opinions expressed in this book are solely those of the author.

The author, Jarred Talmadge, is a licensed Mortgage Loan Originator in the state of Colorado. NMLS License #: 1842043. Jarred Talmadge works for a mortgage company that operates in Colorado. This book in no way makes a representation of Mr. Talmadge's employer.

To check the license status of your mortgage loan originator, visit http://www.dora.state.co.us/real-estate/index.htm. The materials in this book are not from HUD or FHA and were not approved by HUD or a government agency. A reverse mortgage increases the principal mortgage loan amount and decreases home equity. (It is a negative amortizing loan).

Reverse mortgage loan terms include occupying the home as your primary residence, maintaining the home, paying property taxes and homeowner's insurance. Although these costs may be substantial, most lenders do not establish escrow accounts for these payments. However, a set-aside account can be set up for taxes and insurance, and in some cases, may be required by the lender. Not all interest on a reverse mortgage is tax deductible and to the extent that it is, such a deduction is not available until the loan is partially or fully repaid.

Most mortgage companies charge an origination fee, mortgage insurance premium (where required by HUD), closing costs and servicing fees, rolled into the balance of the loan. Most mortgage companies charge interest on the balance of the loan, which grows over time. When the last borrower or eligible non-borrowing spouse passes away, sells the home, permanently moves out, or fails to comply with the loan terms, the loan becomes due and payable (and the property may become subject to foreclosure.) When this happens, all or some of the equity in the property no longer belongs to the borrowers, who may need to sell the home or otherwise repay the loan balance.

Always use your own judgement and/or get the advice of professionals to find the right strategies for your particular situation.

These disclosures are accurate at the time of publication: May 2020.